DON'T GIVE UP!

God is in control

(Prayer series)

Olu Ajala

BALBOA
PRESS

A DIVISION OF HAY HOUSE

Balboa Press books may be ordered through booksellers or by contacting:

Balboa Press
A Division of Hay House
1663 Liberty Drive
Bloomington, IN 47403
www.balboapress.com
1-(877) 407-4847

Because of the dynamic nature of the Internet, any web addresses or links contained in this book may have changed since publication and may no longer be valid. The views expressed in this work are solely those of the author and do not necessarily reflect the views of the publisher, and the publisher hereby disclaims any responsibility for them.

The author of this book does not dispense medical advice or prescribe the use of any technique as a form of treatment for physical, emotional, or medical problems without the advice of a physician, either directly or indirectly. The intent of the author is only to offer information of a general nature to help you in your quest for emotional and spiritual well-being. In the event you use any of the information in this book for yourself, which is your constitutional right, the author and the publisher assume no responsibility for your actions.

Any people depicted in stock imagery provided by Thinkstock are models, and such images are being used for illustrative purposes only.
Certain stock imagery © Thinkstock.

Printed in the United States of America

ISBN: 978-1-4525-7021-1 (sc)
ISBN: 978-1-4525-7022-8 (e)

Balboa Press rev. date: 03/12/2013

For counseling, prayer and preaching
engagement, contact the author.

Pastor Olu Ajala
Christ ambassadors ministries, Inc
P.O.Box 870585, Stone Mountain, GA 30087
Email: info@christambassadors.us
Web: www.christambassadors.us
Tel: 484-919-1489, 770-559-3956

ACKNOWLEDGEMENT

It is my pleasure to acknowledge all readers who have chosen to enjoy peace that Christ has brought for us. The book will channel you to the path of healing for sickness, Grace for race and deliverance for the oppression. It is an expectation that the Holy Spirit will strengthen your faith as you go on your knees to pray over your life challenges. There is an assurance given by Jesus in John 5: 25: "I can guarantee this truth: A time is coming (and is now here) when the dead will hear the voice of the Son of God and those who respond to it will live. Believe it my friend, your miracle is now!

Dedication

To my Wife and the Children

PREFACE

W e are living in an old and dangerous world. Our generation is far aggressive compared with the last century. It will take a fervent believer to survive the challenges of our days. For deliverance to take place, believers must wake up unto a very serious prayer and consistent life.

There is no mountain that cannot become plain, neither a hill that is insurmountable; the way out is to persist and be strong. Do not give up because a quitter has never being a winner. It is just by Fire and by Force. Allow God to take over your situation. He has the power to make things right. Weeping may endure until night but joy comes in the morning. This book is a tool to encourage, teach and to fire you up for prayers that gets results.

Sickness and diseases do not have respect for anyone except the name of Jesus; the name by which all knees must bow and every tongue must confess His Lordship. He has absolute control over everything that He has made. "For by him all things were created, in heaven and on earth, visible and invisible, whether thrones or dominions or rulers or authorities—all things were created through him and for him" Colossians 1:16

This book is not just one of those books, but it was written by the Inspiration of God to meet the specific purpose in your life. It is written to encourage, strengthen and to reiterate the need for you to wake up to prayers on daily basis. We are constantly engaged in the spiritual battles.

Be cheerful "For the weapons of our warfare are not of the flesh, but divinely powerful for the destruction of fortresses" II Corin 10:4 You have been ordained by God to exercise your spiritual authorities as it is written in the book of Jeremiah: "See, today I appoint you over nations and kingdoms to uproot and tear down, to destroy and overthrow, to build and to plant." Jeremiah 1:10 Therefore every plant in your life that is not planted by God must be uprooted and be destroyed. Be it sickness or diseases, bad luck or hereditary problems.

This is not the time to lose hope; this is not the hour to think that your prayers are not answered. It is not the time to turn away from God. This is the acceptable time for you. Your hour of miracles is now! Just believe and you will see the salvation of the Lord.

Perhaps, you are in the sick bed or you are planning to call it a "Quit", may be you are thinking that the loads of problem in your life are unbearable: do not give up; your needed miracle is near you. Take a moment and seek the face of God through the prayer points in this book and your joy will be full.

If your family is going through a rough time today, I want to tell you that there is a God that answers prayer of faith. Believe God, join hands with your family and pray together. God will have mercy upon you. Perhaps you are unmarried or you are a single parent, God has not forgotten you. You may be going through a tough time right now and the sky appears like brass over your head, don't give up; your miracle is on the way. It may be that you are going through a divorce and you feel that you are getting broken down every day; this is not the time to lose the sight of God. Don't give up your courage; tell it over to Jesus. If you have nobody with you at this time; you may be in the sick bed, nursing home, prison or in loneliness; you are not alone, Jesus is just by your side waiting for you to turn it over to Him. You and God are the unbeatable team. Your situations will not crush you if you can turn to God in prayers.

I have experienced the supernatural hand of God on many difficult situations. Jesus has given an open invitation that we should come to Him as we are and He will take our heavy burden and set us free. "Come to me, all you who are weary and burdened, and I will give you rest" Matt 11:28.

I have experienced divine Angelic ministrations couple of times for divine instructions. If God can express His care and love to me in these manner, despite my weaknesses and imperfections, I want to strongly believe with you that your case is also possible.

In the second chapter of this book, I will share with you two real testimonies to encourage you that God can do anything through prayers.

This book is the first edition. More series will follow. You will need handy book like this as your companion. I think it is necessary in order to keep the FIRE on. Remain blessed as you read through.

TABLE OF CONTENTS

CHAPTER 1

Demons have no respect

"For we do not wrestle against flesh and blood, but against principalities, against powers, against the rulers of the darkness of this age, against spiritual *hosts* of wickedness in the heavenly *places*" *Ephesians 6:12*

I have read about series of the miracles that Jesus and the Disciples of Christ performed in the bible, and it is obvious that there are forces of darkness controlled by the demons that specialize in tormenting people through diseases and sicknesses of all kinds. There are untold numbers of nightmares that people are going through as a result of all these fowl spirits.

There was one of my Aunts that got struck in the dream when I was in Africa. She dreamt that she was brushing her teeth and rinsing her mouth with water. At the time of spitting out the water, she just woke up and realized that the real blood was coming out of her mouth. I have to follow my uncle to where she lives. On getting there she was rushed to the hospital and all Laboratory testing performed could not establish any form of infection. She narrated her dream and we realized that it was more spiritual than physical. X-Ray could neither see anything nor was any specific diagnosis arrived at. We took time to pray and bind all blood sucking demons that may be the root cause of bleeding without any etiology. To the glory of God, the blood flow stopped after the prayers. She received her healing after prayer and discharged the same day. Satan has nothing to offer you than calamities if you do not have Jesus. I am not advocating religion but personal encounter with Christ. The scripture says you will know the Truth and the Truth will set you free.

In the course of being in the church Ministry, I have witnessed diverts kind of miracles that God has done in the life of the people; liberating them from all forms of oppressions, depressions, insanity, sickness and diseases. I have heard people confessing that God has delivered them from hearing strange voices. It is obvious that Demons has no respect for anyone. Money, Position, Fame, Being poor or Rich cannot appeal the operation of the demons. The only way out is the way of Truth. Jesus says I am the way, the Truth and the life; no one comes to the Father (God) except by me.

You can begin to wonder, when a child is born, he will look so attractive, tender and appealing. Many of us will appreciate the little "cute" baby. The same child may grow up and become rebellious and addicted to alcohol, drug, street person or all sort of things. What has changed the beauty and innocence of this child? It is not far-fetched . . . Demons have no respect for humanity. Jesus proved this to us times without number in the Bible. Perhaps your home is not settling, your child is no more listening to your directives again, your husband is wayward and you have tried your best to get your family going but your effort is futile. Do not lose hope; your miracle is on the way. This book will open your understanding to the misery of life. Just prepare your heart to pray. If you have never trusted God for anything in the past, why can't you try Him today?

I will like to share with you couple of things to let you know that demons have no respect for anyone except you are a Child of God and redeemed by the blood of the Lord Jesus Christ.

3

Olu Ajala

Healing of a Man Possessed of Demons

"They went across the lake to the region of the Gerasenes. **2**When Jesus got out of the boat, a man with an evil spirit came from the tombs to meet him. **3**This man lived in the tombs and no one could bind him any more, not even with a chain. **4** For he had often been chained hand and foot, but he tore the chains apart and broke the irons on his feet.

No one was strong enough to subdue him. **5**Night and day among the tombs and in the hills he would cry out and cut himself with stones. **6** When he saw Jesus from a distance, he ran and fell on his knees in front of him. **7** He shouted at the top of his voice, "What do you want with me, Jesus, Son of the Most High God? Swear to God that you won't torture me!" **8** For Jesus had said to him, "Come out of this man, you evil spirit!" **9** Then Jesus asked him, "What is your name?" "My name is Legion," he replied, "for we are many."

10 and he begged Jesus again and again not to send them out of the area. **11** A large herd of pigs was feeding on the nearby hillside. **12** The demons begged Jesus, "Send us among the pigs; allow us to go into them." **13** He gave them permission, and the evil spirits came out and went into the pigs. The herd, about two thousand in number, rushed down the steep bank into the lake and was drowned. **14** Those tending the pigs ran off and reported this in the town and countryside, and the people went out to see what had happened. **15** When they came to Jesus, they saw the man who had been possessed by the legion of demons, sitting there, dressed and in his right mind; and they were afraid. **16**Those who had seen it told *the people what had happened to the demon-possessed man—and told about the pigs as well. **17**Then the people began to plead with Jesus to leave their region.*

***18** As Jesus was getting into the boat, the man who had been demon-possessed begged to go with him. **19** Jesus did not let him, but said, "Go home to your family and tell them how much the Lord has done for you, and how he has had mercy on you." **20** so the man went away and began to tell in the Decapolis how much Jesus had done for him. And all the people were amazed" Mark 5:1-20*

You can imagine how the demons can change someone's life style completely. The man that was born one time as a baby with innocent and beautiful nature ended in living in the graveyards. The bible recorded that no one can control this man anymore. This is what happens when you see someone who does not choose the path of righteousness, someone who cannot be talked to. These demons had filled him up to the point that they succeeded in making him to be a lonely person, miserable and rejected. This man did not believe that it can be better for him tomorrow. The people were concerned, they attended chaining him down in order to prevent him from hurting himself but the attempts failed. This man had been a subject of the demons remote control.

There are people in our generation that are so stubborn to the point that there is nobody that can talk to them; they just want everything in their own way. They prefer to live the "Me" kind of life. These are self-centered and isolated people. Many at times they call it "Principle". I will call it a demonic oriented principle. Something is not right somewhere, it is a spiritual issue which over the counter medication cannot resolve. If you have this nature, you definitely need to seek the face of God for help. Such behavior can manifest in anyone if care is not taken. Destroy it in prayer before it ruins your testimonies. God is able to change the heart of rock to the heart of flesh.

However, the man that Jesus healed refused all people that have offered help but because anointing makes a difference, he was able to recognize Jesus. He walked up to Jesus and looked straight to His face. What a compassionate Jesus! He is always being touched by our situations and circumstances. He wants you to come to Him as you are. It does not matter whether you are black or white, confident or coward, great or small, rich or poor. If you can take a step to look unto Jesus in your situation today, He will surely meet you at the points of your need. Many at times you feel like calling it a quit, perhaps you are now thinking of giving up because of what you are going through in your life; this is not the right time to give up, neither would it be an appropriate solution. This is the time to look up to Jesus as this man did. Even if all effort that you have put in place has failed, God will not fail you. All it requires is faith unwavering believing in what God can do.

Jesus knew that the demons that possessed the man have nothing good to offer him. Jesus was full of compassion and he challenged the root cause of the problem. The demons recognized the presence and the voice of Jesus; they knew that the end has come because the one that has the key of life and death has come. Jesus broke the yoke of demonic oppression by sending them out of this man. He severed the connection of the demons from the true nature of this man. As a result, calmness, peace, understanding and deliverance were established. I want to assure you that your case is possible, your joy can be restored, your hope can be revived, your home can be a safe haven, and your children can be great. All you need to do is to turn around and call the name of Jesus on your knees until you hear Him saying "amen" to your request.

A Sick woman (Woman with the Issue of Blood)

__21__ When Jesus had again crossed over by boat to the other side of the lake, a large crowd gathered around him while he was by the lake. __22__Then one of the synagogue rulers, named Jairus, came there. Seeing Jesus, he fell at his feet __23__and pleaded earnestly with him, "My little daughter is dying. Please come and put your hands on her so that she will be healed and live." __24__So Jesus went with him.

A large crowd followed and pressed around him. __25__And a woman was there who had been subject to bleeding for twelve years. __26__She had suffered a great deal under the care of many doctors and had spent all she had, yet instead of getting better she grew worse. __27__When she heard about Jesus, she came up behind him in the crowd and touched his cloak, __28__because she thought, "If I just touch his clothes, I will be healed." __29__Immediately her bleeding stopped and she felt in her body that she was freed from her suffering.

30*At once Jesus realized that power had gone out from him. He turned around in the crowd and asked, "Who touched my clothes?"*

31*"You see the people crowding against you," his disciples answered, "and yet you can ask, 'Who touched me?'"*

32*But Jesus kept looking around to see who had done it.* **33***Then the woman, knowing what had happened to her, came and fell at his feet and, trembling with fear, told him the whole truth.* **34***He said to her, "Daughter, your faith has healed you. Go in peace and be freed from your suffering." (Mark 5:21-34)*

It is extremely ridiculous to be going around with stigma that will dissociate you from a normal life. Here is another example. The demons does not respect any beauty, they can mess you up in a minute when you don't have Jesus as the author of your life. II Corin 5:17 says if anyone is in Christ, is a new creature, old things will pass away and behold all things become new. The woman with the issue of blood went through hell. She spent all that she had, and tried all her possible best. The disease condition was very hard to hide from people because wherever she was, it was the ceaseless flow of blood . . . What a shame?

My friend, it's very important to acknowledge that this woman was in this terrible condition for twelve years. Healthcare was not as advanced as we have it today. Blood loss leads to many complications like various kind of anemia. The woman must have been depleted of Iron level in her blood, the bone marrow and other organs that synthesize blood must have been overworked. Transfusion services were not pronounced at this time if there was any at all. The woman must have also gone through weakness, headache, and loss of orientation, confusion, loss of essential body nutrients, and low oxygen circulation to the tissues and many other complications. Perhaps her family and friends had rejected her.

There is always a time of mercy. The time came when she met her Savior, Jesus Christ the Lord. Consider the faith of this woman *"If I just touch his clothes, I will be healed."* She struggled amidst the crowd just to touch Jesus cloth. She must have stepped on peoples toes to reach Jesus yet she did not give up. Consider what you may be going through today. Think of your rejection and dissociation experience with the people you have loved. May be you are going through a condition that you cannot disclose to people. Do not give yourself stress anymore; there is someone who cares. His name is Jesus. He will make your heart glad.

Guess what! As soon as the woman touched the helm of His garment, the flow of blood stanched. The struggle of twelve years was over immediately. The shame of a dozen year flew away. Instead of being a subject of ridicule as usual, she became a bundle of unspeakable testimonies.

9

There is hope for you. It does not matter how many months or years you have been going through your challenges, if you can exercise faith in the healing power of Jesus; your joy will be full. You might have spent all that you have like this woman, going from one physician to the other. Instead of getting better, it is getting worse. May be you are losing confidence in yourself; perhaps you have been treated wrongfully; lift up your head and behold Jesus. He is fair and compassionate. He is loving and caring. He will give you joy. Pray the following prayers with faith and sincerity of your heart:

Lord Jesus, in thee will I put my hope. I believe in miracle. You are able to heal me as you have healed the woman with issue of blood. Let your power flow into me. Let virtue of your strength heal me. Let there be great open door in Jesus name. I believe that you have healed me in Jesus name. Amen

"Talitha koum!"—Little Girl, get up!

_35_ *While Jesus was still speaking, some men came from the house of Jairus, the synagogue ruler. "Your daughter is dead," they said. "Why bother the teacher anymore?"*

_36_*Ignoring what they said, Jesus told the synagogue ruler, "Don't be afraid; just believe."*

_37_*He did not let anyone follow him except Peter, James and John the brother of James.* **_38_***When they came to the home of the synagogue ruler, Jesus saw a commotion, with*

people crying and wailing loudly. **39**He went in and said
*to them, "Why all this commotion and wailing? The child
is not dead but asleep." **40**But they laughed at him.*

*After he put them all out, he took the child's father and
mother and the disciples who were with him, and went
in where the child was. **41**He took her by the hand and
said to her, "Talitha koum!" (which means, "Little girl,
I say to you, get up!"). **42**Immediately the girl stood
up and walked around (she was twelve years old). At
this they were completely astonished. **43**He gave strict
orders not to let anyone know about this, and told them
to give her something to eat (Mark 5: 35-43)*

What do you expect of Jairus? His only daughter
died of brief illness, the people persuaded him to
give up because his hope was already dashed. Think
about it, at times the people around us compounds
our problems by telling us to desist from looking for
solution. You get written off and they want you to
accept your condition as your fate. We have tendency
to listen to them because of the temporal mental relief.
Jairus did not allow the friends and relatives swerve
him from his faith. He insisted that all he needs is just
a word from Him.

Jesus went with him to his house and He raised the
little girl from death. Note that Jesus was so selective
in His choice of who to follow Him into where the
girl was laid. You need likeminded people in your life;
people that will be able to join hands with you and
pray. You do not need sympathizers or refracts that
will crunch your faith. Show me your friend and I will

tell you who you are. The hope of Jairus family was restored. The family legacy was brought to life again. Your hope can be restored. You are not an outcast. God has designed you for a special purpose. Do not allow any situation to weigh you down. Today, if you will hear the voice of the Lord, then wake up and pray. Fight the battle of faith and in the name of Jesus, victory is sure.

Demons have no respect for the unbelievers and prayerless Christians because there is no fire in them. It is the human nature to put too much thought into what we do and how we feel. We tend to look around for help and when we don't get one, we are overwhelmed. We expect too much from people around us and we tend to put blame on others because we feel that no one cares. It is okay but is not a perfect thing to do. The people around us have their personal issues that they may feel shameful to discuss also. Perhaps they are sharing the same feelings as you did. Stop putting your hope and confidence in people because they are limited. Look up to Jesus, the unlimited in power and grace, full of compassion, and always willing to embrace you as you are. He did it for the woman with twelve years of the issue of blood; He embraced Jairus by raising up his twelve years old girl. He did it for Martha and Mary when Lazarus died in his prime age. He can do it for you today if you have faith unwavering. Remember there is no medication that can heal demon inflicted problems. Use the right tool which is prayer to knock out the devil and his cohorts from their hiding places in your life.

CHAPTER 2

Prayer Saved Mom

Life Testimonies

"Is not my word like fire," declares the LORD,
"and like a hammer that breaks a rock in pieces?
Jeremiah 23:29

1. Deliverance from Small Pox without Medical treatment

"Look, I am the LORD, the God who rules over all flesh. Is anything too difficult for me?" Jeremiah 32:27

This is the first big challenge when I was a teenager. I was going to church like anyone will go to church but I knew I was not born again. My mom was a food vendor and all of a sudden, she was struck with small pox, a contagious disease. Unfortunately, there was no father or relative to come to rescue. It was me and my siblings that she can look up to despite we are high school children.

My mom did not have health insurance neither nor savings reserved for the emergency situation like this. All we grew up to know was her strength in consistent prayer life. I could remember that afternoon when she could not hold her breath again; she called me and my siblings to give us the last words. She encouraged us to take care of ourselves and that she has prayed for us. As a little boy, I was scared because I did not want to lose my mom. I lost my dad when I was Ten years old. There was no member of the family that we can look up to for help except this one "mama" that was struggling tooth and nail to ensure that we become something in life. All the six of us were solely "mama" dependent. Imagine what would have been our fate if God did not answer our prayers. If my mom had passed away through this sickness, I and five others would have become orphans.

Knowing fully well that small pox is a viral infection and it is highly contagious, soberly and with tears running through our little faces, we joined our hands together and leaned on our mom regardless of her painful state and prayed to God for her healing. Jesus said, "Let the little children come to me, and do not hinder them, for the kingdom of heaven belongs to such as these." Matthew 19:14. Don't forget, we came to God as we were, though imperfect and wretched. The omnipotent God who is just waiting for someone to pray and stand in the gap bestowed His mercy upon us. Within 24 hours of our prayers, the small pox dried up, her children did not contract the disease, and she was back on her feet glorifying God for the miraculous healing. I have never seeing a God like the one who saved my mom from this sickness. He speedily answered our prayers as little kids because we only knew at that time that Jesus heals and He can heal our mom.

I do not know your current situation, it may be worse than the small pox infection but here is the word of the Lord for you: He said, "If you will listen carefully to the voice of the LORD your God and do what is right in his sight, obeying his commands and keeping all his decrees, then I will not make you suffer any of the diseases I sent on the Egyptians; for I am the LORD who heals you." Exodus 15:26

If you will listen carefully that every sickness has its spiritual origin, and your way out is to liaise with Him that knows physical, spiritual, emotional and Psychological effect of your current situation, you will seek His face with all your heart. Do not condemn yourself that you are not seriously devoted. Jesus wants to have you as His friend

"What a friend we have in Jesus,
all our sins and griefs to bear!
What a privilege to carry
everything to God in prayer!
O what peace we often forfeit,
O what needless pain we bear,
all because we do not carry
everything to God in prayer.

Have we trials and temptations?
Is there trouble anywhere?
We should never be discouraged;
take it to the Lord in prayer.
Can we find a friend so faithful?
who will all our sorrows share?
Jesus knows our every weakness;
take it to the Lord in prayer.

Are we weak and heavy laden?
cumbered with a load of care?
Precious Savior, still our refuge;
take it to the Lord in prayer.
Do thy friends despise, forsake thee?
Take it to the Lord in prayer!
In his arms he'll take and shield thee; thou wilt find
a solace there.

Charles C Converse, 1832-1918

2. Losing breath from the Sleep

This was a very strange experience from the sleep. It happened to my mom when I was pursuing my first degree in 1991. I came back from the class and I knew that I got enough for the day. I went to bed early tired. At around 2:30 am, I felt strongly from my sleep that someone was pulling my toe. It was pulled so hard to the point that I have to jump up from my sleep. The moment I woke up, low and behold, there was no one in the room. Then I heard a gentle voice speaking into my spirit, start praying for your mom. I was wondering the kind of prayer I should offer and things to pray for. The spirit of God ministered into my spirit that I should pray all manners of prayers. This was an unusual experience. At that point, I realized that when God is about to save His people, He usually send an angel to trigger us to do something. It resembles the time when God was about to wipe of the land of Sodom and He has to rescue Abrahams family from the destruction.

I took the time to pray in the Holy Ghost because He can only help me to pray all manners of prayers. I prayed until I was satisfied and that I have done my due diligence as instructed by God.

I traveled home the following week to see my mom. On getting home, she was narrating her experience that she was losing her breath, gasping for death on the same day and around the same time when God woke me up to pray. She could not explain why it happened and how it happened. I gave all glory to God for His mercies that endure forever.

CHAPTER 3

You and Your Star

What are you going to do today about your life? You cannot continue to assume that everything is just natural. It is time to act by holding God by His words. He honors His words more than His name. God has ordained you to arise and shine because your light has come and the glory of the lord has risen upon you. **Jeremiah 1:10** "See, today I appoint you over nations and kingdoms to uproot and tear down, to destroy and overthrow, to build and to plant."

Isaiah 60:1: Arise and shine, for your light has come and the glory of the Lord has risen upon thee.

The story of the birth of Jesus in Matthew 2: 1-3 is very significant to our lives. When Jesus was born, the wise men saw His star. They saw the star from the East. They saw the rising glory of Jesus at birth and they made all effort to trace where He was being born. You may begin to wonder why the wise men have to be concerned about the unique star after all He was not the only child that was born on that day. Do you know how many wise men and women that have seen your star and are willing to know where you are and what you do? People of great intention, and people like Herod the star killer are out there.

The family of Joseph noticed that he was a rising star and they plotted evil against him. They believe that if they sold him as a slave, his star will never rise. He was maltreated; from pit to Potiphar's house; then lied against and he ended his journey in the prison. However God moved him from prison into praise.

Whatsoever that will quench your light and forbid your star from rising, it has to be fire for fire:

- I am unique! God has made me special! My star is bound to shine!
- I stand against every star gazer of my life in Jesus name.
- The star gazer from birth and after birth
- Every wise man or wise woman staring at my star to crumble in Jesus name.
- I declare blindness to the star gazer of my life in Jesus name.

- Every problem of my life that is connected with my star to give way. Lord! Deliver me from everything that has contaminated my star.
- Every foreign altar that does not allow my star to shine, every obscuring agent that is blocking my manifestation should crumble in the mighty name of Jesus.

The wise people keep watching how you will survive, how you will forge forward, how your dreams will come to pass. These are the key components of Joseph's siblings' attitudes:

- ✓ Joseph's brothers are the wise men of His life.
- ✓ They deliberated from time to time over his dreams and visions
- ✓ They conspired against him
- ✓ They hated him
- ✓ They sold him out
- ✓ They broadcast false report about him

Key prayer points for your life:

- I dismantle the association of the wise men over my life and my star: Associate yourself together you will not stand. Your decree will not hold water over my life
- I command fire and brimstones over every power, group, generation that created time to deliberate over my star in Jesus name
- I turn upside down every form of conspiracy against my life. I declare the enemy of my soul to fall into their own ditch.

- Every tongue that rise against me will fall for my sake
- I disannul every bargaining over my life. Joseph's brother bargained over his future. Let every attempt of the enemy of my star turn to miracles in Jesus name.

Vs. 2: The wise men went to inquire about Jesus in the town where He was born. They moved closer to the people that should know something about you.

- I declare confusion to the way of my star inquirer.
- Generation that wants to monitor where I am and what I do, will not prosper in their craftiness.
- I declare spiritual distortion to their signals in Jesus name

Vs. 3: Herod was troubled, the prince and princess of the land were troubled, and the entire Jerusalem was trouble because a child was born.

How many people were so happy that you were born? How many innocent people have lost their glory into the hands of the wicked one? There are uncountable numbers of people that men of underworld have put in perpetual bondage through food, dream, hand-shaken, snacks and gift exchange. As a person, can you remember all childhood interaction and all sorts of pronouncements over your life?

God did not design the shoe of affliction for you, neither has He appointed you for trouble. He is a merciful God. He cares about what you are going through. All you need to know is the secret of prayer. It works like wildfire.

I heard of the testimony of a man whose star was embedded in the hand of the old woman that took bath for him when he was born. This man went through the elementary, high school, college and he finally got his Ph.D. He sought for job but he could not get any. In the process, he met Christ and gave his life to Him. He had opportunities for employment, and after series of interviews, the result is either "we do not need you" or "you are over qualified". He was in a church program one day when the God opened his eyes that he was going through a spiritual battle. He dedicated time to pray to God. He had a dream one day when God opened his eyes to see a little baby that was born. He recognized the baby to be himself. It was like watch a movie; when he saw this old woman that took bath for the baby. The old lady then took the placenta of this baby and started frying it in the pan. The more she increases the intensity of fire, the more this baby kept on crying. All of a sudden, he saw a very big hand that went into the frying pan and removed the placenta. He realized that the moment this strong hand removed the placenta, the baby stopped crying. Afterward, he woke up from his sleep.

What a tragedy of a wasted life if your star is being tampered with. How long have you been struggling and nothing to show forth?

Your star must shine forth from wherever it is hiding.

God deliberately showed this man the secret of his spiritual battle that he may know the source of his problem. God has delivered him; he got a better job afterward. If God can deliver this man, then your case is possible.

CHAPTER 4

Fire against the Star Killer

Pharaoh traced the Star of Jesus with an attempt to kill Him . . . He made the wise men to be the tracer of the star owner. Who is tracing your star today? What kind of spiritual network has been set up to monitor your star? All spiritual satellites and radars over your life must be destroyed now not tomorrow.

Fire against the Star killers

Jesus birth was foretold. A proof that every child has its own star was when He was born and the wise men were able to recognize His star. You may be wondering if God has known you before birth or not. Jeremiah 1:5 and Isaiah 49: 1 are proves that you are highly favored. A prove that you were made to shine for the glory of God.

Isaiah 49:1-2 "Listen, O isles, unto me, and hearken, ye people from far; the Lord hath called me from the womb; from the bowel of my mother hath He made mention of my name. And He hath made my mouth like a sharp sword; in the shadow of His hand hath He hid me, and made me a polished shaft; in His quiver hath He hid me"

Jeremiah 1:5 "Before I formed thee in the belly I knew thee; and before thou camest forth out of the womb I sanctified thee, and I ordained thee a prophet unto the nations"

If you have not had any encounter with God, this is the time to acknowledge Him. He is your maker and your deliverer. He gave you Jesus as a ransom for your sin and short comings. Accept the simple work of salvation that He has provided as it is written in John 3: 16 For God so loved you that He gave His only begotten Son that if you can believe in Him you will be saved. Accept this offer today by calling Jesus into your heart.

II Corinthians 5:17 says if anyone is in Christ, he is a new creature, old things (sin) have passed away and behold all things will become new to you.

The fact that God knew you from your mother's womb is a wonderful thing to know. God recognized you even when you have not become anything in life. Your current situation is also best known to God.

At this point after accepting Jesus into your heart, no one or any situation is capable of killing your star. Challenges in your life should not overshadow your star. You and God are the unbeatable team. Arise and shine for your light has come and the glory of the Lord has risen upon thee.

When Jesus was born, the wise men saw the star, the star killer (Herod) devised a way of killing the owner of the star but he failed in all his attempts: Matthew 2: 1-3

They wise men saw the star from the East; remember sun rises from the East, The glory of the sun for the beauty of nature. They saw the glory of this child from the distance. It was clearly known that a unique child was born. The wise men made effort to trace where the baby was laid

Jesus was not the only child that was born into the world at that time' but his star was a difference. There is no duplicate you but you will not allow the enemy to duplicate you by changing your orientation to the counterfeit. Why did the situation turn upside down?

Who gazed at your star when you were born as an innocent child? Except you catch the glimpse of this revelation, it will not be meaningful that the star killers are looking for someone they can play like solitar.

It is time for you to arise, and shine! Arise and shine, for your light has come and the glory of the Lord has risen upon thee (Isaiah 60:1). For your star not to shine . . . . It has to be fire for fire!

- *Let all that insist in quenching my star fail without any iota of success.*
- *In all their attempts, let them be confounded*
- *God! Do not let their plans see the light of the day.*
- *I am unique! God has made me special! My star is bound to shine!*
- *I stand against every star gazer of my life in Jesus name.*
- *The star gazer from birth and after birth let the land slide under their feet.*
- *Lord Jesus, let their vision be distorted.*
- *Jesus, let every wicked person, man or woman that is staring at my star crumble in Jesus name.*
- *I declare blindness to the star gazer of my life in Jesus name.*
- *Every problem of my life that is connected with my star to give way. Lord! Deliver me from everything that has contaminated my star.*
- *I declare destruction over every foreign altar that does not allow my star to shine, and over every obscuring agent that is blocking my manifestation in the mighty name of Jesus.*

God dealt with Herod and his people. He killed all that were seeking the life of Jesus. Afterward, God asked Mary and Joseph to return to the land where Jesus was born.

- *Let the rod of the Lord be laid upon they that seek for my downfall.*
- *The word of God says "My soul has escaped as a bird from the snares of the fowlers, so let me escape all the evil plots. Psalms 124: 7*
- *Break the jaws of my enemies and destroy them.*
- *Let the fire and brimstones rain pain and disaster in the camp of they that hate me.*
- *It is written concerning me, touch not my anointed and do my prophet no harm. They that dig the pit before me shall fall into it. They will fill it up with all their assets.*

Vs. 2: The wise men went to inquire about Jesus in the town where He was born. They moved closer to the people that should know something about you

- *In the Mighty name of Jesus, I declare confusion to the way of my star inquirer.*
- *Generation that wants to monitor where I am and what I do, will not prosper in their craftiness.*
- *I declare spiritual distortion to their signals in Jesus name*

Vs. 3: Herod was troubled, the prince and princess of the land were troubled, and the entire Jerusalem was trouble because a child was born.

How many people are so happy that you were born? Many glory had been stolen by helping mother to shower for her baby. There are so many miseries in our lives and so are many questions that remain unanswered. You cannot remember who helped to rub cream on your body when you were young or when you were a baby? It is not possible that you remember them all. Can you remember all their pronouncements over your life? Do you know if you are wearing the shoe of affliction through voodoo? This is the reason why many just walk around with no sign of focus. How many people can tell if they have not eaten the bread/food of affliction that is capable of wiping away the glory and your star? How many contaminated gifts you have received?

Don't be surprised

Your stargazer may be closer to you and you may or may not know. Remember Joseph whose brothers were so mad because of his star. They did all evil under their imaginary power to quench the future plan of God for him. They were bent on making him miserable and disoriented so that his dream may not come to pass. He was put in the dungeon and sold for a token. How many times the people of this world have treated you like a trash? They bent on frustrating you so that you may quit your dream. Tough situation will never last but tough people do. It takes an aggressive prayer to break the aggressive attack of the enemy.

Joseph's brothers deliberated from time to time over his dreams and visions. He was conspired against and they bath him with the soap of hatred. The same blood brothers brought evil reports of him to their father that Joseph had been killed by the wild animal. What could Joseph have done?

- *I dismantle the association of the familiar generations that are working contrary to my life and my star: Associate yourself together you will not stand. Your decree will not hold water over my life*
- *I command fire and brimstones to crash every power, group, generation that created time to deliberate over my star in Jesus name. In the name of Jesus, I turn upside down every form of conspiracy against my life. I declare the enemy of my soul to fall into their own ditch.*
- *Every agent or tongue that rises against me will fall for my sake in Jesus name*
- *I disannul every bargaining power over my life. Joseph's brother bargained over his future. Let every attempt of the enemy on my star turn to miracles in Jesus name.*
- *Let they that are bargaining over my life end up leaking the dust of my feet*
- *Let them be like a carpet under my feet in Jesus name.*

Golden Advice

Apostle Paul said, "Let no man troubles me for I bear the mark of the Lord upon me". Your attitude to your destiny must change from now. Situations have forced you to live in doubt with no grip of your self-esteem. Now is a turning point. Begin to:

1. Walk with your head lifted up
2. Change your perception about life. Aggressively draw a line across your negatives. Turn it to positive.
3. Confess positive and see positive from within you.
4. Success does not jump on you from outside, it begins from within you.
5. When your environment says "NO", let the man inside of you say "Yes".
6. Pray your way into the land of Goshen.
7. Pray until wilderness give way
8. Pray until deserts plants turn green
9. Knowing fully well that you must be engaged in the spiritual warfare. No room for you to be disengaged at any time.

CHAPTER 5

Shake Off the Dust

Your life is in your hand. What you allow to "be" remains with you. God is always "up there", why do you always look down . . . it is a sign of failure and disappointment. You have looked all around you to see if any one may help you but there was none. Have you ever looked up? God is always there! It is time to wake up strong from your dilemma. Shake off the dust that masks your ability to see well.

Shake yourself from the dust

Isaiah 52: 1-6

This is an awakening call: Put on your strength & your beautiful garments: Enough of obscurity! Those things tampering with your beauty must go! Your success blocker must give way. Whatsoever that is chasing away attraction and giving you repulsion must give way. This is your time! Every scale that is covering your beauty must fall off. Your life deserves a beautiful garment.

"For the Lord God will help me; therefore shall I not be confounded: therefore have I set my face like a flint, and I know that I shall not be ashamed. This is the word of the Lord unto me: "Behold, I have made thy face strong against their faces, and thy forehead strong against their foreheads" Ezekiel 3:8 Therefore he that contends against me shall fall, challenges in my life shall crumble in the mighty name of Jesus Isaiah 50:7

No uncircumcised and the unclean will be able to come into your life again.

- Many are weak today because the spiritual strength had been eroded by challenges
- Situation can change your beautiful garment and cloth you with dusty and ugly garments
- Uncircumcised had been your chief counselor
- Your beautiful garments had been removed

- You have put on the garment of sorrow, regret, disappointment and troubles

God says "PUT" on: It is your responsibility with a conscious effort to wake up and determine a change in your life and situations. It is time to shake off the dusts from your life. You cannot wear beautiful garments in the dusts.

What stands as the DUST? Isaiah 29: 5

- Multitude of your strangers shall be like small dust.
- Multitude of the terrible ones shall be as chaff that passes away

Effect of the Dust—Isaiah 29: 4

- They bring you down (Father, I refuse to be down. My talent will not be buried. My future will not be buried. I refuse to be choked by the multitude. Lord Jesus I shake off the dust around me. I am emerging from the dust of life into all newness in Jesus name)
- They make you to speak out of the ground (no Voice)
- They make your voice so low out of the dust

In the mighty name of Jesus, I destroy the plan of my future killer. I destroy every power that is stealing away my strength [physical & spiritual]. No weapon fashioned against me shall prosper. Every tongue that rises against me shall be condemned. Associate yourself together o ye dust of life, thou shall be destroyed. Let there be tornado of the Lord blowing off the dust off your life in Jesus name).

- They are morale killer
- Steal away your confidence

[Lord I refuse the morale killers in my life. I declare beauty for ashes.

Beauty for the dust. I refuse the association of the multitude. I destroy the link between me and the multitude in Jesus name. I am free in Jesus name. Free of the scourge of the tongue at all levels].

Song: Call upon me; in the days of trouble, call upon me, I will answer you

- *Father, I refuse to remain in the dust of life, deliver me from this strange garments*
- *Deliver me from the garment of sorrow and unhappiness*
- *Deliver me from the yoke that have taken away my strength*
- *I refuse to remain weak spiritually*
- *I declare awakening to my soul, spirit and body*
- *I declare my face to be stronger than my situation in the mighty name of Jesus*
- *Vs. 3 . . . . I have sold myself for nothing and so God I shall be redeemed without penalty.*

Claim and possess this: "O thou afflicted, tossed with tempest, and not comforted, behold, I will lay thy stones with fair colors, and lay thy foundations with Sapphires. And I will make thy windows of gates, and thy gates of carbuncles and all thy borders of pleasant stones. And all thy children shall be taught of the Lord; and great shall be the peace of the children. For in righteousness shall thou be established: thou shall be far from oppression; for thou shall not fear: and from the terror; for it shall not come near thee" (Isaiah 54:11-14)

CHAPTER 6

Possess Your Possessions

This is the time for the restoration of your possessions. When God made you, it was a perfect design. There is no out of specification in His design. Whatsoever that is wrong right now is not your portion. You have to get it back on your knees by fire by fire.

Your experience may be for a purpose— It speaks volume of future blessings

Judges 3: 1-2, 3: 12-20

Now these are the nations that the LORD left, to test Israel by them, that is, all in Israel who had not experienced all the wars in Canaan. **It was only in order that the generations of the people of Israel might know war, to teach war to those who had not known it before.** These are the nations: the five lords of the Philistines and all the Canaanites and the Sidonians and the Hivites who lived on Mount Lebanon, from Mount Baal-Hermon as far as Lebo-hamath. They were for the testing of Israel, to know whether Israel would obey the commandments of the LORD, which he commanded their fathers by the hand of Moses. So the people of Israel lived among the Canaanites, the Hittites, the Amorites, the Perizzites, the Hivites, and the Jebusites. And their daughters they took to themselves for wives, and their own daughters they gave to their sons, and they served their gods (Judges 3:1-6 ESV)

There are situations that God allows in your life to prepare and groom you for a purpose. The generation of the warriors whose minds stayed on God were no more in Israel. The younger generations were used to the freedom that their forefathers had fought for. God was not happy to see His favorite getting weak in strength. He decided to train their hands for war by making them to eat with the devils with a short spoon.

Many at times we get wiser and stronger when we face challenges. It makes us to move closer to God. It also happened to the Israelites who did not have the experience of their fore-fathers. God pitched the five most notorious enemies of Israel to live with them. These are the five lords of Philistines who are well experienced at war.

The people of Israel fell into their hands ignorantly and they suffered for eight years. They compromised their faith to the point of marrying the enemies' sons and daughters. They had devils as their in-laws. They worship philistine gods and they forgot God indeed. Sin brings reproach and calamities. When you compromise your trust in God, you are activating troubles and torture. The following can also be some circumstances by which you may be subjected to training:

- ✓ When you have money and you do not know how to manage it and you end up being managed by money . . . . You can be due for God's training.
- ✓ When you have good life and you forget God to serve Him with all your heart, with all your soul and your strength . . . you may be due for training.
- ✓ When God gave you the opportunity to love others and all you can do is to kill them by mouth . . . . May be you are due for the training.
- ✓ When you failed to wait on God to connect you with the right man or woman and you feel that you can just marry someone thinking that you will convert the person to the Lord . . . . You may deserve this training.

39

✓ May be you are currently on training ground; you can graduate today if you are ready for your deliverance.

Can you sincerely answer the following questions?

- Have you been singing God's song in the strange land?
- Have you been eating bread of affliction?
- Have you compromised your faith and have devil as your in-law?
- Have you abandoned God to serve mammon?

You have gone through trials and have failed in strength like the people of Israel. God will like you to rise up in the midst of your challenges like Othneil did. The five lords of philistine took advantage of the unskilled Israelites and dominated their lands, minds and possessions.

Who are the lords of Philistines in your life today that have dominated your marital life, Spiritual, mental and emotional life? It is time to rise up and deliver you like a row. If God has allowed you to go through a tough situation, it is NOW that you have to graduate and have your freedom. Let it click in your heart that your deliverance is now!

1. Have you compromised your faith as a result of trials?

   a. Pray and ask for the forgiveness of your sin
   b. Pray and let God know that you are returning to Him like a prodigal son did.

2. You cannot continue to eat the bread of affliction: Fight affliction and the troubles in your life in prayer. Every spirit of affliction and disaster must give way in your life.

   a. Face it now or you remain in bondage as a prey!
   b. Fight it now and become a winner!
   c. Crush it now in the name of Jesus and you become a Victor!
   d. Bulldoze it in prayer and experience what freedom is!

You do not need any specialist to address your case . . . . It only requires you on your knees. Your challenge does not require a seer but a battle that can be resolved in aggressive prayers. You cannot continue to fold your arms. If you have a snail's speed to act on your situation, your resolution time will be as the speed of a tortoise. Stop twisting your tongue; fight your battle as an experienced warrior. You had enough training to make you pray and pray through. Get on your knees and possess your possessions. Take it back from the thieves and let them pay back in seven folds.

It is time to fight Eglon and his allies in your life: Judges 3:12-14

"And the people of Israel again did what was evil in the sight of the LORD, and the LORD strengthened Eglon the king of Moab against Israel, because they had done what was evil in the sight of the LORD. He gathered to himself the Ammonites and the Amalekites, and went and defeated Israel. And they took possession of the city of palms. And the people of Israel served Eglon the king of Moab eighteen years" (Judges 3:12-14 ESV)

Eglon possessed the core of success and wealth. Palm trees are ever flourish, plant that has never bowed to drought. This is an ever green plant come rain and sunshine. Why should the righteous be enslaved? This is the time to take back all your possessions.

Go on your knee and pray on this prayer points:

- *From the time you have loss the ownership of your peace; you have been paying some dues: Father, I want my Peace back. Have mercy upon me and restore my peace. Your peace is better than the world gives, restore my peace O Lord*
- *The day you loss the possession of your finance, you have been under the mercy of EGLON: Gold and silver belongs to the Lord. Father who has power to bring money out of the mouth of the fish, you are able to connect me to the source of wealth that can never dry.*
- *Take me to the fountain of financial solutions this coming month. Let the land begin to yield increase for me.*
- *I reject lack and financial crisis in my life. Financial crisis brings sorrow and gnashing of teeth. Father in heaven, break the yoke of financial handicap over my life.*
- *I destroy my covenant with lack and poverty in Jesus name.*

- *I destroy every connection to the world of shame and helplessness in Jesus name.*
- *The day you lose your credibility, Eglon of your life has made you a tooth pick: Tonight, I will fight my battle and I will win in Jesus name*
- *God let my credibility be restored by your grace*
- *The land is the Lord's and the fullness thereof, I declare a new name, a new credit for my life in Jesus name.*
- *Eglon's thought towards the people of God is that they have failed, they are now powerless, they are now servants, they have no more credit as a triumphant nation; Father I disagree with all Eglon's notions about my life. That counsel will not stand, that feeling will not see the light of the day. I am stepping into a new life, a new credit, a new victory, in the mighty name of Jesus.*
- *The bible says Eglon was very fat, over the resources of the powerless.*
- *Every Eglon that is draining my life will come down in Jesus name*
- *I command the comfort of my enemy over me to seize in Jesus name*
- *I destroy the slavery spirit over my life. He that worked must eat and enjoy the fruit of his labor. Every power that is draining my resources must die off in Jesus name.*
- *Eglon created a relaxation room while the one that will feed him his bursting his life in the field: I declare the summer room of my oppressors to become their grave yard*
- *Every power that is militating against my existence must bow in Jesus name*

- *Every generation that is betting on my success will be put to shame in Jesus name.*

Eglon possessed the City of Palm trees: For 18 years, this man was enjoying while the rightful owner of wealth were living from hand to mouth.

- *I am returning to the city of palm trees today in the mighty name of Jesus.*
- *God, rend your heavens on my behalf, let there be a change of status today in Jesus name*
- *God has to give you a new song from now on, a new history, a new chapter of Success and accomplishment in Jesus name.*

1. Palm tree is beautifully designed by God

- *From now on my life will be beautiful at all levels*

2. Unique among all trees, no regular branches, always grow tall among the peers

- *Father you have carefully made me when no one knows. Let that uniqueness radiate gloriously*
- *My glory must not be covered. My light must shine and darkness shall not be able to comprehend it.*
- *Let everything about me bring glory to you; not shame; neither disappointment; failure, pain, nor tears on your altar every time.*

- *Let the uniqueness of the Lord in my life strengthen me on daily basis, that my life will usher praise to the throne of grace every day of my life.*

3. **Nothing is a waste but everything on palm tree is very useful**

- *God my life must not be a waste. Enrich me father. Pray that Lord should enlarge your coast and broaden your horizon.*
- *Refuse to be a waste to humanity. Your life is not a trash to reckon with. Refuse to be as dirt to human race. Let your light shine and let the glory of the Lord be risen upon you.*

4. **Palm trees are used for shelter:**

- *Make me a shelter for many generations. Establish me as a resource that will never run dry.*
- *Make me a resource for people. Help me to leave unforgettable and positive legacy in the life of men*
- *Help me with all resources of life and strengthen me to affect my generation and generation to come positively*

5. **Palm trees are all season Fruitful:**

- *Bareness is forbidden in all areas of my life in Jesus name. I must be fruitful so I forbid bareness of the womb, marital bareness, financial bareness, spiritual bareness and all forms of lack in my life*

- *If you are barren of good life, you will be full of sorrow; Father, I reject every form of bareness in Jesus name*

6. **Palm trees live longer than any tree. Behold palm trees competes with human life span:**

- *God, I declare in the mighty name of Jesus that you will satisfy me with long life. My sun will not set at noon.*
- *My years will not be cut short neither would I live in sorrow in all my years in the name of Jesus.*
- *I bind and subdue every spirit of pre-mature death in the name of Jesus. I forbid it in my family and relatives. I declare a divine shield from God to envelope and my households in Jesus.*
- *I declare long life and prosperity in Jesus name*

7. **Palm tree is well rooted, strong and tough.**

- *I will be well rooted with good life in Jesus name.*
- *I will be well rooted in the work and service of God in Jesus name. I will not fall by the way side neither would I be found wanting in the presence of God at all times.*
- *I reject weaknesses, sickness, failures, shady life style, confusion, and all events*

challenging my strength and my existence in Jesus name.

8. Drought is no barrier to its existence

* *Palm tree is all weather plant and it is ever blossom. I declare my life to be blossoming, radiant and be full of grace in Jesus name.*

9. These resources attracted Eglon and he did possess it. Vs 18-20

* *It is not too late to possess all that God has ordained for me. Ehud knew that it is time to rebound.*
* *It is time to rebound: You have struck the hard surfaces of your life; it is time for you to rebound. Today, the only option is to rebound to success; your possession; your manifestation, and it's now! Not tomorrow.*
* *Time to re-possess my city of palm trees. I declare my time of fulfillment to manifest in the name of Jesus.*
* *Time to restore my peace and Health; I receive my healing and I declare restoration of my health in the mighty name of Jesus*
* *Time to regain my credibility: I declare my glory restored in the name of Jesus. Every stone that has been rolled to block my manifestation, I address in Jesus name to be crushed.*

- *Bye forever to lack: I severe my relationship with poverty and lack. I break the chord of union between I and the spirits of poverty in Jesus name*

CHAPTER 7

Breaking the Chains

"The thief comes only to steal and kill and destroy, I came that they may have life, and have it abundantly" John 10:10. Whatsoever that has been stolen from your life; be it health, joy, confidence, self-esteem, hope, home or job; the chain of evil events must be broken. You deserve freedom and now it is available for you through Jesus Christ. Your business must resurrect, your dry bones must receive life and your weeping has to stop because God has delighted in you.

Jesus is the answer to every question that you may have. Weeping may endure until night but joy comes in the morning. Psalm 30: 5b. You have worked for years and there is nothing to show forth. You have tried various business but all have failed. Perhaps you have gone back to school in order to improve your skills and it has not made any difference. The good news for you is that there is a God that cares who will embrace with mercy.

Remember Lazarus who had died for four days before Jesus got to his tomb but Jesus raised him up. Would you critically examine the story of Lazarus and learn more about God divine principle? John 11:1-44

Lazarus lived in Bethany of Judea and named the friend of Jesus. The reality of life is that if you are a friend of God or a child of God, it does not exclude you from earthly challenges. The unwavering assurance is that Jesus will take care of you. Lazarus situation was worse; he was sick and died. The entire family members and neighbors were broken down because Jesus did not show up on time. Martha and Mary said "Lord, if you have been here, my brother wouldn't have died" and Jesus said, "Your brother shall rise again".

Does it really mean anything to you? Are you losing hope on anything? Are you giving up at this time? Dear friend, your hope is not lost. Your situation will be better.

You can effect a change in your situation if you can remember to invite Jesus as Mary and Martha did.

There is a King whose voice the dead hears; whose presence makes the earthquake. He is the King that has the key of hell and death; He can open and no one can close. His name is Jesus. When He opens your grave, He will cause you to rise again.

Jesus commanded people to roll away the stone that was blocking the exit door to live. You may not know what is blocking your way of success, promotion and blessings but the truth is that the stone has to give away. Address the situation in your life with prayer today. Fight the battle of faith and victory is sure.

Bound hand, Feet and Face

The three major physical parts of human body designed to carry out activities are the hands, feet and eyes. When Lazarus died, there was no more hope for freedom. They made it a "case closed" for this young man. Jesus could see beyond the physical; He could see that

- Lazarus feet will still walk
- Lazarus hands will still hold the blessings
- Lazarus eyes will still behold great things
- Lazarus life will become a unique testimony

What can you see today? What can Jesus see in you today? You can still walk! Arise in the name of Jesus and begin to walk. Declare your body to receive a new strength from God in Jesus name. Your miracle is for now and not tomorrow. Physicians cannot write you off, friends and relatives cannot write you off, perhaps your spouse has put you in the "Ground Zero" thinking that you will not be able to rise again. You will surely rise in Jesus name!

Hands are essential to live. If your hands are spiritually bound, there is no amount of money that you make that stays with you. Break the yoke of all spiritual handcuffs that are limiting you. Jesus said to them, "Loose him, and let him go". Lazarus hand, feet and face received freedom by the authority of Jesus. Divine resurrection and encounter is what you need today.

There is no reason to remain in a confined situation like grave. There is no freedom in grave. No opinion. No social life style. You can't grow taller than the size of the grave. You cannot move hands and feet in the grave. Grave is a locked up dungeon, sealed and cemented. No light in the grave but total darkness. You lay down in stagnancy. Today, the chain of the grave of life must be broken: Here are some prayer points for your devotion:

- *Lord Jesus, let your resurrection power quicken my mortar body*
- *Let every stone that blocks my success and breakthroughs roll away*
- *By His word "Loose Him let him go", Lazarus was set free from the bondage of death; Declare the chains and fetter sin your life to be broken; and let every bound be lose.*
- *If Lazarus can resurrect by your word, I will resurrect, my business will resurrect, my relationship with God will be quickened*
- *My future will be bright*

- *Grave is full of darkness but in your case, the light and the glory of God will be for you and your household.*
- *My family will awake from the position of redundancy into a glorious place*
- *Lazarus found favor in the sight of God, so shall the mercy and grace of God abide with you and the household in the name of Jesus.*
- *Destroy every barrier to your resurrection*
- *Every embargo to your resurrection: Destroy it*
- *Every negative pronouncement about your life must be neutralized by the blood of Jesus*
- *Jesus said, "Lazarus, come forth" (3-letter words is what you need to come out of your predicament)*
- *I loose myself from every veil that covers my ability to see the way out of my dungeon*
- *I loose myself from the bondage that wraps my hand and my feet*
- *I destroy every restriction power to my destiny*
- *I liberate myself by the power of Jesus from every dead situation*

Here is another reason why God has to attend to resolve your case:

Matthew 27: 62-66; 28: 1-4

The soldiers sealed and guarded Jesus's tomb. The king forbid any rescuer, no friends or relatives must been seen moving near the tomb. The plan was to make Him decay in the grave and avert the foretold resurrection. The Priests and Pharisees

- Petitioned Jesus when He was alive as seen in John 11:45-57
- Petitioned His dead body as seen in Matthew 28:62-66
- Petitioned His plan to resurrect after three days, Matthew 12:40; 16:21

Who has been petitioning your life? Perhaps people are petitioning your existence. People around you petition your views and opinion; they make you miserable and isolated. It may be that you have become the talk of the town and the music of ridicules in their mouth. One thing you have to know is that, if the host of heaven can rise to defend Jesus course, your case is much simpler because you will laugh last.

Psalm 102: 9—"For I have eaten ashes like bread, and mingled my drink with weeping" Psalm 30:5b—"Weeping may endure for a night, but joy comes in the morning". We face challenges that cause us to weep and weary our souls. At times, we just want to shut down and close up our minds. You may be going through this process right now just as David said . . . Eaten ashes like bread; a cup of water mingled with tears running into it. You might have been weeping over an issue for years or months; perhaps your expectation is falling off the cliff and your hope is getting dashed every day, do not vex, your miracle time is now.

Look at how people ganged against Jesus. The church leaders in Bethany before and after the resurrection of Lazarus in John 11 planned to arrest Him and kill

Him for their selfish reasons. These are the "to know" people. They shared faith with Him, knowledge of the scripture and professed spiritual mentors. Close friends, relatives or church members can stand to be heart brokers. Always remember that you cannot change any man but you can only manage their behaviors. Your help is not from what people can offer; it has to come from God who literally gives it without expecting a return. Jesus said that He has given us peace not as the world giveth it. Therefore, do not lean on people to prevent sudden crash. People have high tendency of expressing pain when you depend on them but God never. God cares, loves and strengthens; make Him the first resource for all your concerns.

God asked Ezekiel a reality check question in Ezekiel 37:1-6 and this is applicable to us today. Consider situations that appear like dry bones in the valley. Solid as rock and hard as bones are some problems that we go through. God sees our situations in a different way. He will like you to see it as rootless events. There is power in the spoken words. For your challenges to be resolved, God needs your input. Your input must be objective and not subjective. It must come with a positive mind that God is able to make it happen for you. You cannot be whining every day and twisting your tongue over the same issues forever, it is time to hold the bull by the horns and trust God for His help.

*[3] He asked me, "Son of man, **can these bones live?**" I said, "Sovereign LORD, you alone know." ⁴ Then he said to me, "**Prophesy to these bones and say to them, 'Dry bones, hear the word of the LORD!** ⁵ This is what*

55

*the Sovereign LORD says to these bones: **I will make breath**[a] **enter you, and you will come to life.** 6 I will attach tendons to you and make flesh come upon you and cover you with skin; I will put breath in you, and you will come to life. Then you will know that I am the LORD."*

Can God resolve your pain? Can all that appear as dry bones in your life live? Do you really trust the intervention of Jesus?

Think about this, can God resolve your marriage? Can He give you the forgiving spirit? Are you willing to soft-pedal on your decision? Do you hope for a great change? All these are possible but it will begin with you. God knew that the dry bones can live before He asked Ezekiel but miracle will not happen until Ezekiel makes himself available and share a common thought with God. No Matter what you are going through today, God absolutely understands but He requires your attention and inputs to get it resolve.

You have to make up your mind that you are ready for God's action. If you find it difficult to forgive people for their misconducts and heart-felt situations, God can help you now. All you have to do is to have a positive mind of readiness to forgive. Pray for the grace of God to love people as they are, not as you really want them to be. When you exchange love for hate, it does not mean that you are "cheap" or "weak" but you are actually "expensive" and "strong" because you have gotten attribute that many sought to have. This is priceless and worth more than gold. The question is Can you do it? Yes! You can.

God asked Ezekiel if the dry bones can live and he agreed with God that it is possible. Then God asked him to "prophesy" that *"Dry bones, hear the word of the LORD!"*

This is not a passive language against the dry bones. You do not have to address every situation with a passive tone. It calls for aggressive prayers. For our struggle is not against flesh and blood, but against the rulers, against the authorities, against the powers of this dark world and against the spiritual forces of evil in the heavenly realms—Ephesians 6:12. You cannot afford the sickness to cage you. Address all forms of sickness and diseases that have names in the name of Jesus. Call it by its names and declare the word of the Lord against it as Ezekiel did to the dry bones. It is written "That at the name of Jesus every knee should bow, of things in heaven, and things in earth, and things under the earth"—Philippians 2:10

So I prophesied as I was commanded. And as I was prophesying, there was a noise, a rattling sound, and the bones came together, bone to bone. ⁸ I looked, and tendons and flesh appeared on them and skin covered them, but there was no breath in them.

⁹ Then he said to me, "Prophesy to the breath; prophesy, son of man, and say to it, 'This is what the Sovereign LORD says: Come, breath, from the four winds and breathe into these slain, that they may live.'" ¹⁰ So I prophesied as he commanded me, and breath entered them; they came to life and stood up on their feet—a vast army

Pray all manners of prophetic prayers over your life and the family. Declare what has not happened to come to being. Let all closed doors open up by the word of the Lord. It requires Prayer action, faith and perseverance because by strength, no man shall prevail. Speak to the situation of your life to receive the breath of life and the power of God Ezekiel 37:5 "I will cause breath to come into you and you will live".

The following scriptures may help to get you started:

You need the voice of the Lord: *"The voice of the LORD twists the oaks and strips the forests bare. And in his temple all cry, "Glory!"* **Psalm 29:9**

Let the voice of the Lord come into your life and strip the forests that are blocking your joy and freedom. You are ordained to be part of the worshippers that shout, "Glory to God for His mercy endures forever"

All gates have to shift that you may be able to pass. Every barrier has to collapse. Every closed door has to open. Why? Because the King of glory has come: Psalm 24: 7-10

*"**7**Lift up your heads, O you gates; be lifted up, you ancient doors, that the King of glory may come in. **8**Who is this King of glory? The LORD strong and mighty, the LORD mighty in battle. **9**Lift up your heads, O you gates; lift them up, you ancient doors, that the King of glory may come in. **10**Who is he, this King of glory? The LORD Almighty—He is the King of glory".*

The Lord will fulfill His plans for your life this year. Do you know why? Because He made you! Psalm 138:7-8 "*7 Though I walk in the midst of trouble, you preserve my life; you stretch out your hand against the anger of my foes, with your right hand you save me. 8The LORD will fulfill [his purpose] for me; your love, O LORD, endures forever—do not abandon the works of your hands*"

The world hung Jesus on the cross that you may receive your healing. He has perfected your healing over 2000 years ago. All you need is simple, know and acknowledge His stripes have made you whole. Confess this and you will receive your healing in Jesus name. Isaiah 53:5 "*But he was wounded for our transgressions; he was crushed for our iniquities; upon him was the chastisement that brought us peace, and with his stripes we are healed*"

Many other scripture verses may be of help for your situation. Look for a bible and start developing relationship with God. Let the word of God dwell in you richly as written in Colossians 3:16 "*let the Word of the Messiah, in all its richness, live in you, as you teach and counsel each other in all wisdom, and as you sing psalms, hymns and spiritual songs with gratitude to God in your hearts*"

CHAPTER 8

After All said and done: God still loves

For God so loved the world that he gave his one and only Son, that whoever believes in him shall not perish but have eternal life John 3:16

Y ou cannot imagine the depth of the love of God to you and your family. People may reject you because of whom you are but this God will embrace you as you are. It does not matter whether you are poor or rich, great or small, alcoholic or non-alcoholic, gay or straight. Just come to Him as you are and he will save you. He will deliver you from the bondage of sin. John 3:16

For all have sinned and fall short of God's glory Romans 3:23. You cannot deliver yourself from the power of sin. Consider the number of times you have tried to change your behavior but you are still repeating it. You really want to move closer to God but the world keeps pulling you back. If you neglect the love of Christ to deliver you, sin will sting and kill you and you will end up in hell. Your life is precious to God and that is why He is giving you another opportunity to repent of your ways and turn unto God.

Jesus said "Behold, I stand at the door, and knock: if any man hear my voice, and open the door, I will come in to him, and will sup with him, and he with me" Revelation 3:20

Would you open the door of your heart today? Let us face the truth; your ways have not brought any joy or long lasting happiness. Many at times you feel confused and hopeless. Parties, drink, cracks cannot bring peace but has brought troubles and anguish of heart. Dear friend, "If you hear God speak today, do not be stubborn. Don't be stubborn like those who rebelled." Heb. 3:15

Do not condemn yourself because there is no exception. We all, like sheep, have gone astray, each of us has turned to his own way; and the LORD has laid on him the iniquity of us all. Isaiah 53:6 God has laid your sin on Christ Jesus that you may be free. I was a run-away person like you in the past until I decided to receive the love that God as offered through Jesus. You need directives, guidance and help from God from time to time. Hand your life over to Him and He will take care of you. You have received enough failure and disappointments from people. Why can't you try Jesus today? He bears your feelings and concerns. He is a perfect shepherd for your soul.

Jesus gave it all to you through His death and resurrection. That is why salvation is an open door and it is free for all the people that cherish freedom. "He was delivered over to death for our sins and was raised to life for our justification" Romans 4:25. If it is not real, I will not be confident to pass it on. It is a live testimony through personal experience that the love of God is real and undiluted. Apostle Paul confessed—"For what I received I passed on to you as of first importance: that Christ died for our sins according to the Scriptures" (I Corinth 15:3)

Jesus has been a sacrifice for our sin. One sacrifices for us all which has brought healing, deliverance from the power of sin and the joy of eternal glory with God. What a great gift from God! What a great privilege! "He himself bore our sins in his body on the tree, so that we might die to sins and live for righteousness; by his wounds you have been healed" 1 Peter 2:24

One thing is very clear, "If anyone is in Christ, he is a new creation; the old has gone, the new has come! II Corinthians 5:17 There is provision for a new experience when you give your heart to Jesus. This is the result of a personal encounter with Christ Jesus. He is the gate that leads to peace and life. He is the author and the finisher of our faith. Your response to His invitation can restore your hope and joy. It is a 360^0 turning point.

How?

1. Acknowledge that you are a sinner
2. Confess your sin to God in your prayer
3. Ask for the forgiveness in the name of Jesus
4. Tell Jesus that your heart is open for Him to enter
5. Pray that God should strengthen you not to go back to your old nature
6. Ask Holy Spirit to guide your heart from now on
7. Promise God that you will change completely
8. Thank God for forgiven your sin
9. At this point, if you are sincere to the steps you have taken, then you have become a child of God.
10. Get a bible for your daily devotion. You may start from the book of John. God will help you to understand more of Him through the Bible
11. Find a church to attend because faith comes by hearing the word of God.
12. Do not hesitate to ask believers questions, you won't have full understanding of everything

immediately. I Peter 2:2 Like newborn babies, **crave** pure spiritual milk, so that by it you may grow up in your salvation

Perform a reality Check

How your life does looks like before Christ? What is it after Christ? Share your testimonies with others that they may consider Jesus for their life situations.